Dung beetle's dinner

by Clint Twist

Copyright © ticktock Entertainment Ltd 2006

First published in Great Britain in 2006 by ticktock Ltd.,

Unit 2, Orchard Business Centre, North Farm Road, Tunbridge Wells, Kent, TN2 3XF

We would like to thank: Elizabeth Wiggans and Dr John Walters for their help with this book.

ISBN 1 86007 840 0 PB Printed in China

A CIP catalogue record for this book is available from the British Library.

Picture Credits

Corbis: 22c and 31t, 23t. FLPA Images: 2-3, 4t, 11bl, 12-13 all, 14-15 all, 17 all, 20, 21t, 29b.

Image Bank: 16-17 main. PhotoDisk: 18-19 main, 20-21c.

We would be pleased to insert the appropriate acknowledgements in any subsequent edition of this publication.

CONTENTS

What are dung beetles?

Dung beetles are medium-sized winged insects. They can be seen rolling balls of dung (animal waste) along the ground. They often fall over, and are sometimes called tumblebugs.

How do dung beetles live?

A dung beetle lives in an underground burrow that it has dug. Males and females usually live in separate burrows. In some species the males look quite different to the females, with horns on their heads.

What do they eat?

Dung beetles feed on the dung of large plant-eating mammals that graze on grass or browse on the leaves of trees and shrubs.

A dung beetle feasts on cow manure in Australia.

A giant dung beetle rolls a ball of dung in the Addo National Park, South Africa.

Where do they live?

Dung beetles live anywhere where cattle, buffalo, horses, antelope and other large mammals are found.

A pair of brightly coloured male and female dung beetles from South America.

Understanding minibeasts

Insects belong to a group of minibeasts known as arthropods. Adult arthropods have jointed legs but do not have an inner skeleton made of bones. Instead, they have a tough outer "skin" called an exoskeleton that supports and protects their bodies. All insects have six legs when they are adults, and most also have at least one pair of wings for flying, although some have two pairs.

All beetles belong to a group of minibeasts known as arthropods.

THE DUNG BEETLE UP CLOSE

The average dung beetle is about 40-70 mm long and has six legs and only one pair of flying wings. It is divided into three parts – head, thorax, and abdomen.

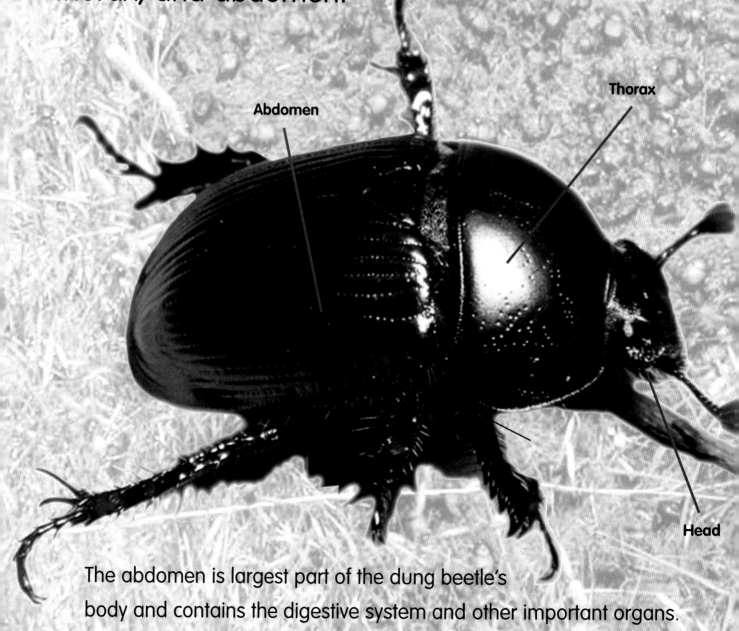

Thorax

Abdomen

Head

The abdomen is largest part of the dung beetle's body and contains the digestive system and other important organs.

Beetles have only one pair of flying wings – the back pair. Instead of front wings, they have a pair of stiff, hardened wing cases that are called elytra.

The opened elytra reveal this dung beetle's flying wings.

When the beetle is on the ground, the elytra fold over the flying wings. When the beetle is flying, the unfolded elytra stick out to provide additional lift.

The head is equipped with antennae, eyes, brain and mouth. The thorax is the middle part of the body and the legs and wings are attached here.

Six Legs

Beetles and other insects are sometimes called hexapods because they all have six legs (hex means six in Latin). This is correct, but it is not completely accurate. All insects are hexapods, but not all hexapods are insects.

Dung beetles have six legs like all other hexapods.

A World of Dung

Dung is the solid waste material produced by plant-eating mammals. Plants are a much less concentrated form of food than meat. Plant eaters have to eat much larger quantities than meat eaters, which means they make large amounts of solid waste.

For dung beetles, and many other minibeasts, the dung of plant-eating mammals represents a vital supply of food.

No animal has a digestive system that is 100% efficient and there is always some part-digested plant material in dung, together with dead bacteria and useful minerals.

Large plant eating animals such as elephants leave large piles of dung!

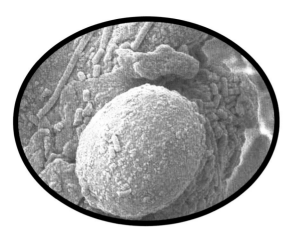

A magnified view of bacteria inside a dung pile.

When dung is left on the ground, tiny plants and fungi from the air and soil begin to grow on the part-digested material.

Fungi such as Psilocybe coprophila grow only in dung, providing food for dung beetles.

It is these tiny plants and fungi, which will grow only in dung, that are the dung beetle's main source of food.

Clean-up crew

Dung beetles and other dung-eating insects are part of nature's vast, but largely unseen, clean-up crew. Without these millions of minibeasts, the world's grasslands would become covered in a layer of dung. Other members of the clean-up crew get rid of dead bodies. Sexton beetles, for example, bury the bodies of small mammals and birds so that their young can feed on the corpses.

Sexton beetles are often called burying beetles because they bury the corpses of small animals.

Something Smells Good

The smell of dung attracts dung beetles. The greatest numbers of dung beetles are found in places where there are the largest numbers of plant-eating mammals – areas of grassland such as the Serengeti Plain in Africa.

While huge herds of mammals are passing through the Serengeti Plain in Africa, there is an abundance of dung. Beetles in search of a meal do not have to walk very far.

Wildebeast graze on the plains of the Serengeti in Africa.

In scrubland, however, mammals are few and far between and their dung is very scarce. A fresh dropping attracts dung beetles from up to 800 metres away.

Dung is scarse in scrubland such as this plain in Namibia, Africa.

Beetles do not have noses. Instead they use their antennae to take samples of the air. A dung beetle's antennae can detect the very faintest traces of the smell of dung.

Antennae

Best way to travel?

Like most other animals, beetles normally travel headfirst. Their eyes and sense organs are located on the front of the head where they can probe the unknown in the direction of travel. This might seem very simple and obvious, but as we shall see with the dung beetle – headfirst is not always the best way to travel.

The scoop-shaped head of a South-American dung beetle.

Dung Mining

Minibeasts take a variety of different approaches to a pile of dung - some tunnel straight in to find the best bits, while others are content just to nibble at the edges. Dung beetles are not generally too fussy about quality.

Dung beetles are superbly designed and equipped as dung miners. A strong, curved head shield (left) protects the front of the head.

The edge of the head shield has notches like the teeth on a mechanical shovel.

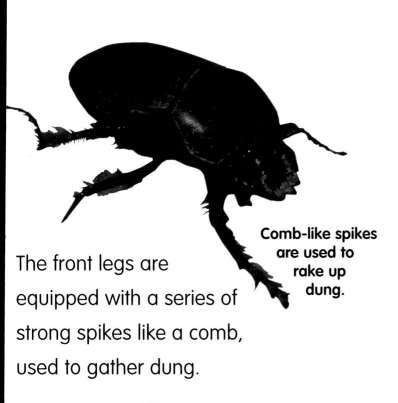

The front legs are equipped with a series of strong spikes like a comb, used to gather dung.

Comb-like spikes are used to rake up dung.

The beetle then uses its body to press the dung into a tightly packed, solid ball.

The weight of a dung beetle helps to shape the dung into a compact ball.

Solo achievement

No matter how hard they work dung beetles can never match the amazing achievement of termites, which are the mining, construction and engineering champions of the insect world. Termites build earthen mounds more than 4 metres high with tunnels beneath that extend about the same distance underground. But it takes millions of termites to build a mound – one termite by itself can do very little – while each dung beetle's ball is a solo achievement.

A termite mound in Namibia, Africa.

Shaping the Ball

As a dung beetle collects more and more dung with its front legs, the compressed ball beneath its body gets bigger like a snowball being rolled along in the snow. Eventually the ball gets so big that the beetle is tilted forwards.

Powerful legs help the dung beetle grip the ball and stay steady during the rolling process.

In this strange position, the dung beetle then uses its middle legs and back legs to make the ball even bigger.

These legs have tiny hooks on the ends that allow the beetle to get a good grip on the ball of dung.

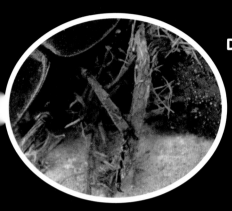

Dung beetles have hooks on the ends of their legs to help them cling on to the dung ball.

The beetle can then turn the ball this way and that, to ensure that every bit of the surface has had the same amount of pressing between the insect's body and the ground.

Insect engineering

When human engineers want to measure the size, shape, and smoothness of a ball, they use an instrument called a pair of callipers that has two pieces of curved metal hinged together at one end. The middle and back legs of a dung beetle act like two pairs of natural callipers that enable the beetle to make precisely shaped dung balls of exactly the right size.

The positioning of the legs of a dung beetle allow it to roll perfect balls of dung every time.

Rolling Home

When it is satisfied with the size and shape of its dung ball, the beetle can start pushing the ball straight back to its burrow. The beetle starts walking in a straight line, paying no attention to the slopes and curves of the ground.

The dung beetle makes this return journey while walking backwards, because its front legs are useless for controlling the ball. It takes all four middle and back legs to steer the ball in a straight line.

Walking backwards in a straight line over bumpy ground is difficult even without pushing a massive ball of dung.

A pair of European dung beetles struggle to push a ball up a steep sand bank.

Mishaps and setbacks happen with nearly every journey, and its frequent falls have given the dung beetle an alternative name - the tumblebug.

The colourful Ischiopsopha dung beetle.

Muscle power

Although the dung beetle might seem to make very slow and uneven progress, it is usually successful – and this success represents a triumph of insect muscle power. When the beetle pushes a dung ball across 100 metres of grassland, it is equivalent to a person pushing a small car cross-country for three kilometres over rough ground that is covered by thick jungle.

Pushing a dung ball over rough or grassy ground is an exhausting experience for a dung beetle.

Underground Larder

Sometimes the tasty dung ball is eaten as soon as the beetle gets back to its burrow. Often, however, the dung ball is stored in the burrow to provide food for times when fresh dung is scarce.

In many places dung is scarce all year round, and even on the best grassland it can become scarce at times. For example, when the vast herds of mammals on the Serengeti migrate to fresh pastures the amount of dung available for dung beetles drops dramatically.

Wildebeast prepare to migrate from the Serengeti Plains, Africa.

The inside of a dung ball remains quite damp and sticky.

Fortunately for the dung beetles, a well-rolled dung ball will stay edible for several months.`

Although the outside of the ball may dry out, the dung in the middle of the ball will stay quite damp and the tiny fungi and plants inside will continue to grow.

Cradle of dung

After mating, a female dung beetle carefully makes a special egg ball, choosing only the very "best quality" dung. She takes extra care on the homeward journey to make sure the surface of this ball is completely smooth. Inside the burrow she lays her eggs in the middle of the ball, with just a single air hole so that the eggs can breathe.

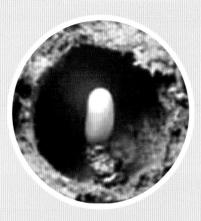

A single dung beetle egg inside a burrow.

caring Mother

Among many dung beetle species, the females stay in the burrow with their eggs, guarding them against predators and parasites. In the world of minibeasts there are many species that specialise in feeding on the eggs of other species – just as among larger animals there are many that feed on birds' eggs.

The developing larvae of a dung beetle.

If the female is successful, her eggs will soon hatch and grub-like larvae will emerge. The larvae begin to feed on the tiny plants and fungi inside the ball.

A female dung beetle introduces her young to a dung ball.

They remain inside their cradle of dung until after they have pupated and acquired the adult body shape.

The pupa of a dung beetle recovered from inside a burrow.

When the small beetles have eaten their way out of the dung ball, the patient female escorts them up out of the burrow. Once on the surface, she introduce them to their wonderful world of dung.

Insect development

Insects develop from eggs in two different ways. With many kinds of insect, the eggs hatch into larvae that look very different from the adults. The larvae go through a stage called pupation when they change into adults. However, with many other kinds of insect, such as cockroaches and grasshoppers, the eggs hatch into nymphs that already have the adult body shape.

At the end of the dung beetle's larval stage the larva create a pupation cell. Alternatively they find a safe place to go while their bodies change into pupa.

Dung Beetles & Humans

The Ancient Egyptians believed the dung beetle was a sacred insect. They called it a scarab, and that name is still used today. The scientific name for dung beetles is Scarabaeidae, and they are often referred to as scarabid beetles.

The Ancient Egyptians saw young beetles emerging from apparently dead balls of dung and thought that this was a miraculous creation of life.

They also believed that a scarab pushing its ball across the ground represented the Egyptian gods pushing the Sun across the sky.

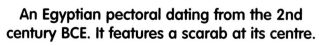

An Egyptian pectoral dating from the 2nd century BCE. It features a scarab at its centre.

Many people wear good luck charms (below and left) in the shape of a scarab made of wood, stone, pottery, or glass.

In some parts of the world, dung beetles are protected by people. This sign in KwaZulu, Natal, South Africa, warns people to watch out for passing dung beetles.

The success of failure

In many ways, dung beetles are most useful when their efforts fail (due to disease, natural disaster or lack of food) when the stored food remains uneaten, or the eggs fail to hatch. All the millions of uneaten dung balls represent a very efficient method of mixing animal dung into the soil. Dung is a very good fertilizer for land (farmers call it manure), and when dung beetles fail in their own purposes, they do succeed in fertilising the land so that the grass continues to grow.

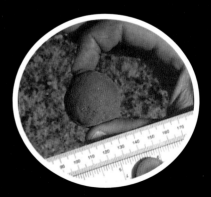

Unused dung balls help to fertilize the land, adding nutrition as they rot.

Dung Beetle Variations

There are thousands of species of dung beetles in different parts of the world. They all have the same basic shape, and follow the same basic patterns of behaviour, but there is a considerable amount of variation in the details.

Precious metals

Most dung beetles are quite dull in appearance, but some from tropical regions are very eye-catching. On the "precious metal scarabs" from South America (right), the elytra and the top of the head have a bright, shiny gold or silver appearance.

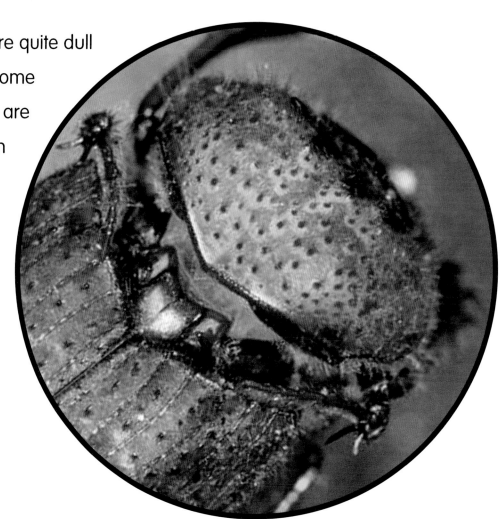

Labour-saving beetles

Most dung beetles collect their dung from large
piles left by large mammals, and they have
to work hard cutting and shaping each
dung ball. Other dung beetles, such as the
European minotaur beetle, have a more laid-
back approach. They specialise in collecting the
dung of rabbits, which exactly the right size and
shape for dung beetles and is ready to just roll away.

Too big to bury

In India, there is a species of dung beetle that
rolls a dung ball much larger than normal –
the size of an apple or orange – and much
too big for the insect to bury. Instead, the
beetle carefully coats the ball with a thick
layer of mud. After the mud dries, it keeps the
dung inside quite fresh and damp.

No rolling

Not every species of dung beetle collects dung balls.
Aphodian dung beetles, which are only about 5 mm long
when fully grown, tunnel into the soil beneath suitable
deposits of dung. Once the burrows are dug, aphodian dung
beetles can then feed whenever they want in complete safety from
predators such as birds.

other Beetles

T here are more species of beetles than any other insect – scientists already know of about 400,000 – and new beetle species are discovered almost every day. Among the other main sub-groups of beetles are:

Fireflies

Despite their name, fireflies are actually beetles, and they are also called lightning bugs. They are found in woodland and grassland regions throughout the world. These beetles have special organs on the abdomen that produce flashes of green light. Each species has its own pattern of flashes, which is used to attract mates.

Weevils

This is the biggest group of beetles and there are more than 40,000 known species. Weevils are also known as snout beetles because they have a narrow head that ends in a long snout. The jaws are positioned at the end of the snout. Most weevils are plant-eaters and some species, such as the cotton-boll weevil, are serious agricultural pests.

Diving beetles

Diving beetles are some of the fiercest predators found in ponds and streams. The great diving beetle (shown right feeding on a fish) is about 50 mm long and can seize fish of even greater size in its powerful jaws. When they dive beneath the surface, diving beetles trap air beneath the wings and between the hairs on the abdomen.

Ladybirds

These dome-shaped beetles are easily recognisable by their distinctive pattern of spots. Some species, such as the seven-spot ladybird, always have the same number of spots, while others, such as the convergent ladybird, can have any number between 2 and 13. Ladybirds are popular with gardeners because they eat insect pests

Find out More
Lifecycle

Most dung beetle species reproduce in spring, summer and autumn, when the weather is warmer. In some species, the female and male work together to dig a burrow and bring dung into the home - in others these duties are just performed by the female. A female dung beetle will then lay eggs in the burrow which will hatch into larvae. These larvae eventually develop into pupa. As they feed on dung brought into the burrow, they grow into adult beetles, and dig their way to the surface.

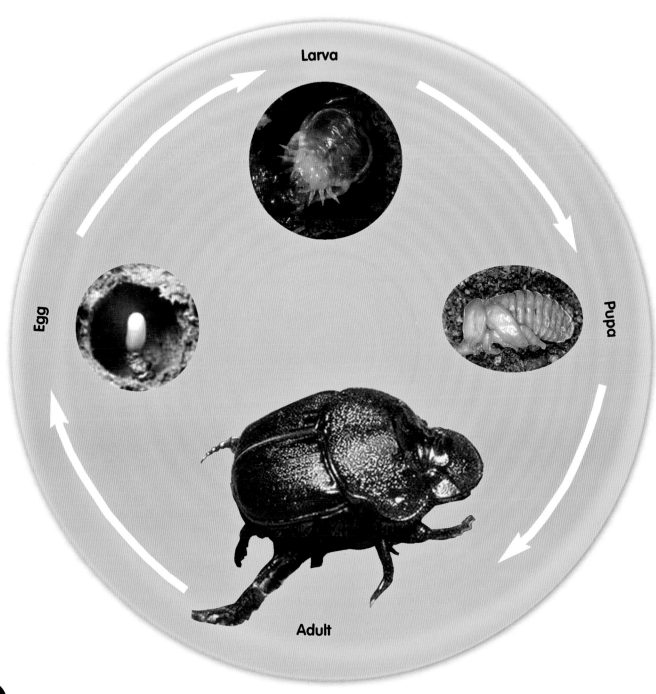

Larva

Egg

Pupa

Adult

Fabulous Facts

Fact 1: Dung beetles are a relatively modern group of beetles. The oldest fossils date back only 40 million years.

Fact 2: Scientists have found 6,000 species of dung beetle. Some specialise in one type of animal dropping.

Fact 3: One species of dung beetle, for example, spends most of its time stays on a sloth. When the sloth's droppings fall, the beetle drops onto the dung.

Fact 4: In 1973 an incredible 16,000 dung beetles climbed onto a 1.5 Kg pile of elephant dung on the African savannah in just 2 hours.

Fact 5: Dung beetles were imported into Australia by farmers to stop flies breeding. By eating cattle dung, these beetles deprived the flies of fresh dung to breed in.

Fact 6: One dung beetle can bury 250 times its own weight in a night.

Fact 7: New research suggests dung beetles use moonlight at night to roll a dung ball to a safe spot.

Fact 8: Some tribes from South America believe a dung beetle named Aksak modelled the first man and woman from clay.

Fact 9: Some dung beetles like our poo! Onthophagus caenobita has only ever been found feeding in human faeces.

Fact 10: Dung beetles range from less than 1mm to a giant 6cm.

Fact 11: A dung beetle in South America called Zonocopris gibbicolis feeds on the droppings of large snails. It rides around on their backs waiting for the waste to drop!

Fact 12: Some dung beetles eat and lay their eggs on dung other beetles collect. They also eat the dung owners' eggs as well as stealing their dung.

Fact 13: Dung beetles occur on every continent except Antarctica. The life expectancy for most dung beetles range from three to five years.

GLOSSary

Abdomen – the largest part of an insect's three-part body; the abdomen contains most of the important organs.

Antennae – a pair of special sense organs found at the front of the head on most insects.

Arthropod – any minibeast that has jointed legs; insects and spiders are arthropods.

Bacteria – microscopically small organisms that can live just about anywhere; some bacteria cause disease.

Beetle – one of a large group of mainly ground-dwelling insects; there are more than half a million species of beetle.

Calliper – an instrument used by engineers to measure the diameter of spheres and cylinders.

Coprophagic – the scientific term that describes a "dung-eating" animal.

Digestive system – the organs in the body that are used to process food.

Dung - the solid waste material produced by the digestive systems of plant-eating mammals

Elytra – the stiff, hardened wing cases that protect the flying wings of beetles.

Exoskeleton – a hard outer covering that protects and supports the bodies of some minibeasts.

Fungi – (singular fungus) a group of living things that are separate from plants and animals. Fungi range in size from microscopic yeasts to large toadstools and mushrooms.

Insect – a kind of minibeast that has six legs, most insects also have wings.

Jaws – hinged structures around the mouth that allow some animals to bite and chew.

Larva – a wormlike creature that is the juvenile (young) stage in the life cycle of many insects.

Mammal – one of a group of warm-blooded animals that have an internal skeleton and which feed their young on milk.

Minerals – natural substances found in rocks and soil that are essential for both plants and animals.

Minibeast – one of a large number of small land animals that do not have a skeleton.

Nymph – the juvenile (young) stage in the life cycle of insects that do not produce larvae.

Organ – a part of an animal's body that performs a particular task, e.g. the heart pumps blood.

Parasite – any living thing that lives or feeds on or in the body of another living thing.

Predator – an animal that hunts and eats other animals.

Pupa – An insect larva that is in the process of turning into an adult.

Pupation – the process by which insect larvae change their body shape to the adult form.

Scarab – the Egyptian Ancient name for a dung beetle, the name sometimes used today to refer to any dung beetle.

Serengeti – a large area of tropical grassland in East Africa.

Skeleton – an internal structure of bones that supports the bodies of large animals such as mammals, reptiles, and fish.

Thorax – the middle part of an insect's body where the legs are attached.

Tumblebug – the popular name for a dung beetle.

index

A
abdomen 6, 26, 30
adult insects 5, 21, 28
Africa 5, 10–11, 13,
    18–19, 29, 31
Ancient Egyptians 22–3
antennae 7, 11, 30
Aphodian dung beetles
    25
arthropods 5, 30
Australia 4, 29
B
bacteria 8–9, 30
balls of dung see dung
balls
beetles
    types 26–7
    understanding 30
burrows 4, 16, 18–21,
    25
burying beetles 9
C
callipers 15, 30
clean-up insects 9
coprophagic animals 30
cow dung 4, 29
D
digestive system 6, 8, 30
diving beetles 27
dung 4, 8–11, 30
dung balls
    homeward journey
16–17
    India 25
    larvae 20–1
    moonlight rolling 29
    shaping 13–15
    storing 18–19
E
eggs 19, 28, 29

Egyptians 22–3
elephant dung 8, 29
elytra 7, 24, 30
European dung beetles
    17, 25
exoskeleton 5, 30
eyes 11
F
females 4, 5, 19–21, 28
fertilizer 23
fireflies 26
fish 27
flies 29
food 4, 8–9, 18–20
fossils 29
fungi 9, 19, 30
G
giant dung beetles 5, 29
good luck charms 22–3
grassland 10, 31
H
head 6–7, 11, 24
head shield 12
hexapods 7
homeward journey
16–17, 19
hooks, legs 15
humans 17, 22–3, 29
I
Indian dung beetles 25
insects
    clean-up insects 9
    development 21
    hexapods 7
    mining insects 12–13
    understanding 5, 30
Ischiopsopha dung beetle
    17
J
jaws 27, 30

K
KwaZulu, Natal 23
L
ladybirds 27
larvae 20–1, 28, 30
legs 5, 7, 13–16
life expectancy 29
lifecycle 28
lightning bugs 26
lucky charms 22–3
M
males 4, 5, 28
mammals 4–5, 8–11,
    18–19, 25, 30
manure 23
meat eaters 8
minerals 8–9, 31
minibeasts
    understanding 5, 31
    see also insects
mining insects 12–13
minotaur beetle 25
moonlight 29
mud-coated dung balls 25
muscle power 17
N
Natal 23
nymphs 21, 31
O
Onthophagus caenobita
29
organs 6, 11, 26, 31
P
parasites 20, 31
plant eaters 4–5, 8–11,
18–19, 25
precious metal scarabs 24
predators 20, 25, 27, 31
protecting dung beetles
    23

pupa 21, 28, 31
pupation 21, 31
R
rabbit dung 25
rolling dung balls 14–17,
    29
S
scarabs 22–3, 31
scrubland 11
sense organs 11
Serengeti 10, 18–19, 31
Sexton beetles 9
shaping dung balls
    13–15
skeleton 5, 31
sloth droppings 29
smell 10–11
snail droppings 29
snout beetles 27
South America 5, 11,
    24, 29
species of dung beetle
    24–5, 29
spikes, legs 13
steering dung balls
    16–17
storing dung balls 18–19
T
termite mounds 13
thorax 6–7, 31
'tumblebugs' 4, 17, 31
V
variations, dung beetles
24–5, 29
W
weevils 27
wildebeast 10
wings 5, 7
Z
Zonocopris gibbicolis 29